DISABLED DOGS

by Meish Goldish

Consultant: Janet Van Dyke, DVM
Diplomate, American College of Veterinary
Sports Medicine and Rehabilitation

New York, New York

Credits

Cover and Title Page, © Robert F. Bukaty/Associated Press; Cover TR, © Aaron Alexander; Cover CR, © Brandi Simons; Cover BR, © Doug Beghtel/The Oregonian; TOC, © Stephanie Lindemann/Cougar Ridge Photography; 4, © Jude Stringfellow; 5, © Splash News; 6, © Brandi Simons; 7, © Patrick Nugent, SMSgt, USAF (Ret.); 8, 9, © Tricia Simpson; 10, 11A, © Doug Beghtel/The Oregonian; 11B, © LAMB / Alamy 12, © Kathy Beer; 13, © Jim Rydbom; 14, 15 © The Kaufman Family; 16, 17, © Leslie Grinnell; 18A, © Oak Hill Animal Rescue; 18B, 19, © Richard Allen Schlossberg; 20, 21, © Jim Mahoney/The Dallas Morning News; 22, © John Welsh; 23, © Gary Roberts/Rex USA/BEImages; 24, © Aaron Alexander; 25, © Getty Images/Staff; 26, © Ellen Levy Finch; 27, © OrthoPets V-OP Veterinary Clinic; 28, © Lindsey Mladinich; 29A, © Erik Lam/Shutterstock; 29B, © phloxii/Shutterstock; 29C, 29D, © Eric Isselée/Shutterstock.

Publisher: Kenn Goin
Senior Editor: Joyce Tavolacci
Creative Director: Spencer Brinker
Design: Dawn Beard Creative
Photo Researcher: We Research Pictures, LLC

Library of Congress Cataloging-in-Publication Data

Goldish, Meish.
  Disabled dogs / by Meish Goldish.
    p. cm. — (Dog heroes)
  Includes bibliographical references and index.
  ISBN 978-1-61772-697-2 (library binding) — ISBN 1-61772-697-4 (library binding)
  1. Dogs with disabilities—Juvenile literature. I. Title.
  SF992.D46G65 2013
  636.7'0897712—dc23

                              2012032978

For more information, write to Bearport Publishing Company, Inc., 45 West 21st Street, Suite 3B, New York, New York 10010. Printed in the United States of America.

10 9 8 7 6 5 4 3 2 1

Table of Contents

Keeping Faith

In 2002, when a puppy with golden fur was born, her owner noticed something unusual. The tiny puppy, named Faith, was missing one of her front legs. Her other front leg was badly bent, leaving her unable to walk. Reuben Stringfellow, a friend of the dog's owner, felt that he could give Faith the extra care that a dog without a leg would need and brought Faith home. Reuben worried, though, that the little puppy might never walk on her own.

Faith's bent leg had to be removed to prevent further health problems.

As Faith grew older, the Stringfellow family tried to teach her to walk on her two back legs. Yet Faith would always fall down. All that changed, however, the day that Faith discovered her favorite food—peanut butter. To urge Faith to walk, the family placed peanut butter on a spoon and called out her name. Instantly, she began to hop toward the treat, bouncing along on two legs like a kangaroo!

Dogs may be born with a disability or they may become disabled after a serious illness or injury.

Faith walking with Reuben's mother, Jude Stringfellow

Inspiring Others

With practice, Faith became skilled at walking and running on two legs. She quickly proved to the Stringfellows that she wouldn't let her **disability** hold her back. Jude Stringfellow, Reuben's mother, wanted to share Faith's inspiring story with others. So she took Faith to visit hospitals and nursing homes, where she brought joy and hope to people with disabilities.

Faith and Caity Stringfellow, Jude's daughter

Over time, Faith developed stronger muscles in her hind legs and hips to help her walk on two legs.

Jude also took Faith to visit several U.S. **military bases** around the country. During her visits, Faith inspired American soldiers leaving for or returning from war. "She shows what can be achieved against great odds," said Jude. Faith was even made an **honorary** sergeant in the U.S. Army for helping lift the spirits of disabled war **veterans**.

Faith visits two U.S. Army soldiers.

Leading the Way

Dogs that have disabilities, such as Faith, have an incredible ability to **adapt** to life. Tricia and Stan Simpson learned this after they **adopted** Echo, a blind Australian shepherd. At first, they worried that their new dog might have trouble getting up and down the stairs. So Tricia led Echo to a steep staircase to help him get used to it. He carefully felt the edges of the first three steps with his paws as he slowly climbed each one. Minutes later, Echo was racing up and down the entire staircase on his own!

Despite being born blind, Echo has learned how to jump through hoops.

Echo also learned how to locate things in the Simpsons' home by using his senses. He used his nose to sniff out food treats each morning. Using his sense of hearing, he played hide-and-seek with the family's daughters. Echo showed the Simpsons that a blind dog can still be an active and playful pet.

Echo with the Simpson daughters, Piper and Hunter

Blind dogs can **memorize** where objects are in their homes. This helps them find things, such as their food bowl, and move around without falling down stairs or bumping into furniture.

Best Buddies

While some blind dogs can get around easily on their own, others need a helper. Diego, a Chihuahua, lost his sight at age five in a coyote attack. After that, a pug named Kona, who lived with Diego, became his **guide**. Diego followed Kona everywhere. When Kona died a few years later, Diego grew sad and slept most of the time.

Diego (right)

Diego's owner, Clarice Keating, knew that her dog needed a new pal and guide. So she adopted another pug, named Buddy Nixon. In a short time, the Chihuahua learned to follow the sound of Buddy's jingling collar and his nails tapping on the floor. It was now much easier for Diego to find his food bowl and the way to the yard. He also had a new best friend.

A bell on Buddy's collar, such as the one shown here, helps Diego hear where Buddy is.

Clarice chose another pug as Diego's companion because pugs are often noisy. Their flat faces cause them to breathe loudly, which makes it easy for blind dogs to hear them.

Clarice with Diego and Buddy Nixon

Amazing Angelyne

With a little help from their owners, disabled dogs like Diego can lead happy lives. Some owners, however, don't realize at first that their dogs have disabilities. When Eric Melvin adopted a puppy named Angelyne, he could not understand why she did not follow **commands** in **obedience** class. So Eric took her to a **veterinarian**, who soon discovered the problem.

Eric Melvin with his Australian cattle dog, Angelyne

The vet explained to Eric that Angelyne is deaf and cannot hear voice commands. As a result, Eric taught her to follow hand signals, which she can see. The **canine** quickly learned more than 40 hand signs. Despite her disability, Angelyne dances and performs tricks. She not only amazes people, she makes them smile.

Angelyne often visits schools for deaf and **hearing-impaired** children. "She let me know that humans aren't the only ones that have hearing problems," one student said. "Animals do too."

Eric uses hand signals to teach Angelyne tricks, such as jumping through a hoop.

Wheels That Heal

Disabled dogs sometimes need special **equipment** in order to lead full, active lives. Kodi, a Great Pyrenees, loved to run and play outdoors—until he got sick. At age ten, he developed a disease that caused his hind legs to collapse whenever he stood or walked. His owner, Cindy Kaufman, wanted to help Kodi get around on his own, even with his disability.

Kodi loves to be near people.

Cindy found an Internet site called handicappedpets.com. There, she learned that many disabled dogs can be fitted with a **harness** and wheels to help them walk and run. Within weeks, Kodi had a Walkin' Wheels dog wheelchair. It took him only a short time to get used to the equipment. Now he uses it to play outside every day—even in the snow!

The rolling equipment that allows a disabled dog to walk is often called a wheelchair, cart, or wheels.

Kodi gets around easily with his new wheels.

On a Roll

Many companies make specially made wheelchairs for dogs. Company workers consider many things when they make their equipment. To be sure the wheelchair is the right size for the dog, its designers must know the animal's height, length, and weight. They must also know what type of disability the dog has.

Disabled dogs, both large and small, use dog wheels.

Besides making wheelchairs, companies sell items such as booties that the dog may also need to safely get around. Disabled dogs often drag their **paralyzed** feet on the ground as they walk. As a result, they need to wear the rubber booties to protect their delicate paws.

A dog using a front-wheeled cart

Doggy wheelchair companies build wheels for dogs that do not have use of either their back legs or their front legs.

Rubber dog booties

To the Rescue

Two dogs that zip around on their wheels are Chili and Arlo. Each dog needed help getting around for a different reason. When Chili was a puppy, someone threw her over a fence. The fall broke her back and left her unable to use her hind legs. Arlo has a disease that paralyzed the back part of his body, causing him to drag his rear legs behind him.

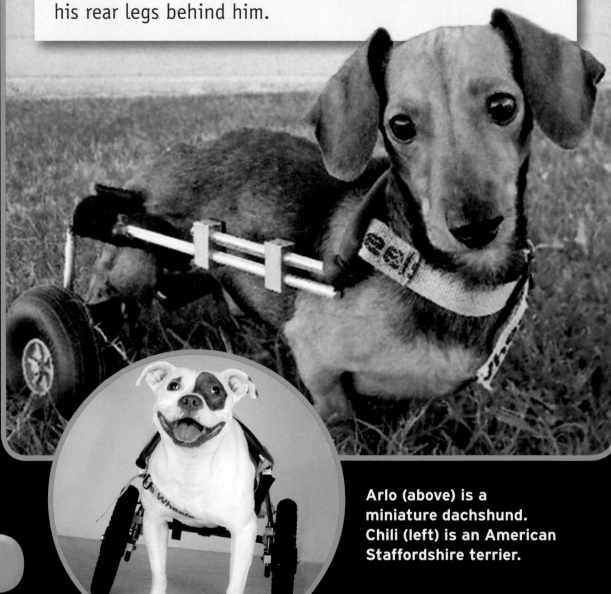

Arlo (above) is a miniature dachshund. Chili (left) is an American Staffordshire terrier.

Luckily, both dogs were rescued by Jim and Bettye Baker. They run the Oak Hill Animal Rescue in Seagoville, Texas. The couple had wheels built for both dogs. "The minute we put Arlo in the chair, he took off like a rocket," Bettye said. It took a little longer for Chili to get used to her wheels, but "now she absolutely flies!"

Chili and Arlo with their owners, Jim and Bettye Baker

Since 2006, Jim and Bettye Baker have found families for more than 500 homeless dogs. However, they decided to raise Chili and Arlo themselves after falling in love with them.

A Popular Pair

Thanks to their wheels, Chili and Arlo can go just about anywhere. One of their favorite places to visit is the Baylor Institute for **Rehabilitation** in Dallas, Texas. There, they work as **therapy dogs**. They visit disabled people who are just learning to use wheelchairs. On seeing the inspiring pair, many patients say, "If those dogs can do it, so can I."

Arlo snuggles up with a young patient at the Baylor Institute.

Chili and Arlo bring out the best in people. "The patients just love them," said their owner Jim Baker. Sometimes the dogs help patients heal faster. One ill man had been unable to move his right hand for five days—until Chili rolled up to him. "Without thinking, I reached out with the right hand!" said the grateful patient.

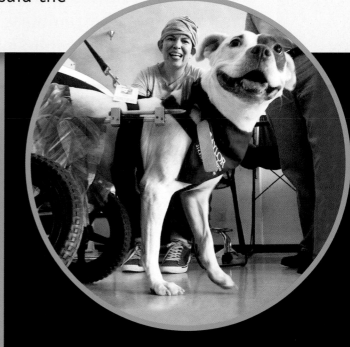

With her wide grin, Chili cheers up a disabled patient.

Linda Marler, program director at the Baylor Institute, says that visits from dogs such as Chili and Arlo make patients happier, healthier, and more relaxed. "It helps to decrease their need for pain medication and lowers their heart rate," said Linda.

Finding a Home

Chili and Arlo live with a loving and caring family. Other disabled dogs, however, are not so lucky. Because dogs with disabilities require extra care, some owners give them up and often place them in shelters. Dogs that are not adopted at shelters may be put to sleep.

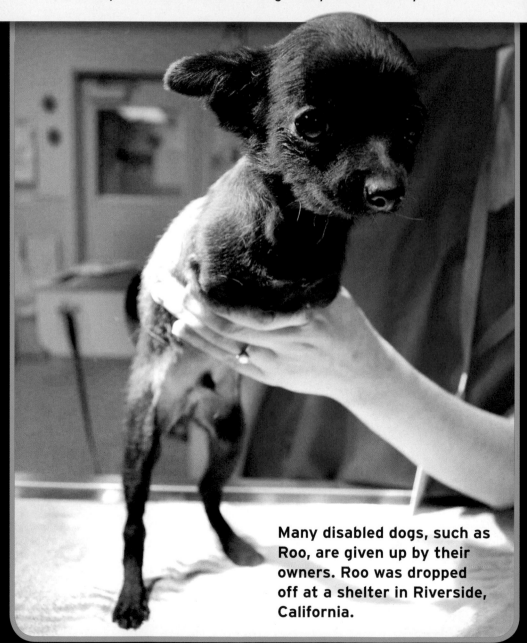

Many disabled dogs, such as Roo, are given up by their owners. Roo was dropped off at a shelter in Riverside, California.

One organization that helps find homes for disabled dogs is Pets with Disabilities. It's run by Joyce Darrell and her husband, Michael Dickerson. They began their work in 2000 after their dog, Duke, broke his back in an accident. Since then, the couple has rescued dozens of disabled pets from shelters. They then help find people who are willing to adopt these animals and give them loving and caring homes.

These three disabled Chihuahuas were rescued from a shelter.

In addition to finding homes for disabled pets, Joyce and Michael provide information, support, and advice for people who already have disabled pets.

Special Care

Caring for disabled dogs isn't always easy. Sometimes, pet owners aren't sure how best to handle their dogs. Luckily, groups such as Pets with Disabilities are able to offer advice. They explain how to care for a disabled dog, depending on its specific needs.

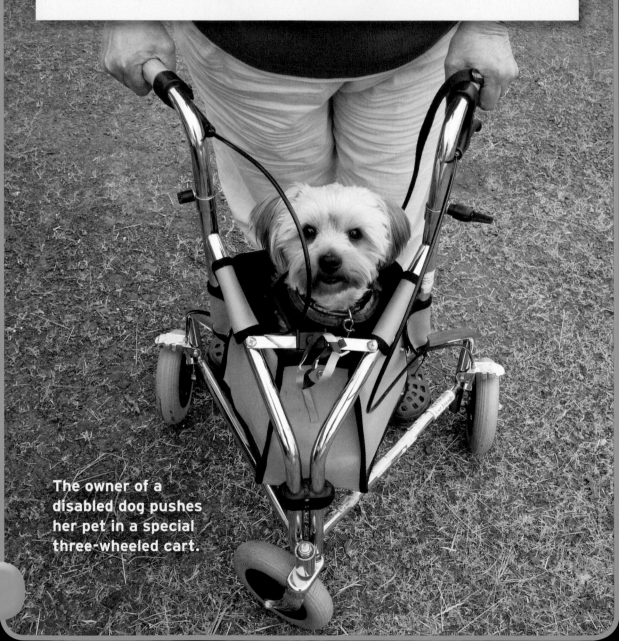

The owner of a disabled dog pushes her pet in a special three-wheeled cart.

For example, owners of blind dogs should keep the animals' path clear of items that they might bump into. Also, blind dogs rely mainly on their strong sense of smell to find their way around. According to dog expert Caroline D. Levin, blind dogs, "can almost see with their nose." As a result, it's helpful for owners to dab perfume on doors and walls so the animals can use the scent to recognize where they are.

Some blind dogs wear special glasses, called Doggles or doggie goggles, to protect their eyes from injury.

Because blind dogs memorize their surroundings, owners should keep all household furniture in the same place at all times. Also, owners should use soft pads to cover any sharp corners on furniture that a blind dog might run into and be injured by.

Perfect Pets

What else can people do to keep their disabled pets healthy and happy? Some owners of deaf dogs put **vibrating** collars on their pets. Whenever the owner wants the animal's attention, he or she presses a button to make the collar gently tingle. That way, the dog can "feel" when he or she is being called.

A deaf dog wearing a vibrating collar

Because deaf dogs cannot hear moving vehicles or other dogs, it's important to keep them on a leash or in a fenced yard.

Dogs with special needs often amaze people with their ability to adapt to just about any situation. With the right care and equipment, disabled dogs can live long, happy lives. As Faith and the other disabled dogs prove, with a little help and a lot of love, anything is possible.

Naki'o, a dog that lost all four of his paws, jumps into the air.

Just the Facts

- Dogs with wheelchairs can usually travel on all kinds of surfaces, including grass, dirt, sand, and snow. When the dog gets tired of walking, the cart can be removed so that the dog can lie down without it.

- Blind dogs can learn to safely walk in unfamiliar places, as long as their owners walk close beside them and keep them on a leash or harness. Over time, blind dogs learn to use their owners as "seeing-eye people."

- Dogs can lose their hearing for many reasons. Some dogs are born deaf. Others may lose their hearing due to an ear injury or disease, or simply because of old age.

- At North Carolina State University and Fitzpatrick Referrals in Surrey, England, scientists are developing **artificial** limbs for dogs. OrthoPets in Denver, Colorado, also creates specially made leg braces and artificial limbs for dogs.

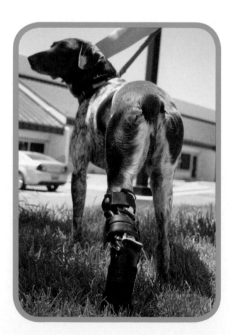

A dog named Brownie with an artificial leg from OrthoPets

Common Breeds: DISABLED DOGS

Any kind of dog can become disabled. Here are several dog breeds featured in this book.

Australian cattle dog

Chihuahua

Dachshund

Great Pyrenees

adapt (uh-DAPT) to change to fit one's environment

adopted (uh-DOPT-id) taken in as part of one's family

artificial (*ar*-ti-FIH-shul) made by a person or machine; something not found in nature

canine (KAY-nine) a member of the dog family

commands (kuh-MANDZ) orders given by someone

disability (*diss*-uh-BILL-uh-tee) a condition of the body that makes it hard to do certain things, such as walking, seeing, or hearing

equipment (i-KWIP-muhnt) the tools and machines needed to do a job

guide (GIDE) a person or animal that leads or shows the way to others

harness (HAR-niss) a piece of equipment that is strapped onto an animal's body and then attached to a wheelchair

hearing-impaired (HIHR-ing-im-PAIRD) not able to hear very well

honorary (AH-nuh-*rare*-ee) given as an honor without the usual requirements or duties

memorize (MEM-uh-rize) to learn something by heart

military bases (MIL-uh-*ter*-ee BAY-siz) centers for armed forces; often places where soldiers live and from which they operate

obedience (oh-BEE-dee-uns) the act of following good behavior and rules

paralyzed (PA-ruh-lized) a body part that can no longer move

rehabilitation (*ree*-huh-*bil*-uh-TAY-shuhn) a process to restore a person or animal to good health

therapy dogs (THER-uh-pee DAWGZ) dogs that visit places such as hospitals to cheer up people and make them feel more comfortable

veterans (VET-ur-uhns) people who have served in the armed forces

veterinarian (*vet*-ur-uh-NER-ee-uhn) a doctor who takes care of animals

vibrating (VYE-brate-ing) moving back and forth quickly

Bibliography

Darrell, Joyce. *Extraordinary Dogs: Inspirational Stories of Dogs with Disabilities.* Guilford, CT: Lyons Press (2007).

Masters, Susan. *Living with a Disabled Dog: Charlie's Story.* Amazon Digital Services (2012).

Shafer, Mary A., ed. *Almost Perfect: Disabled Pets and the People Who Love Them.* Ferndale, PA: Enspirio House (2008).

Read More

Apte, Sunita. *Combat-Wounded Dogs.* New York: Bearport (2010).

Horsky, Nicole. *My Dog Is Blind—But Lives Life to the Full!* Dorchester, England: Hubble & Hattie (2010).

Whitehead, Sarah. *How to Speak Dog!* New York: Scholastic (2008).

Willms, Jennifer. *My Dog Is Deaf—But Lives Life to the Full!* Dorchester, England: Hubble & Hattie (2011).

Learn More Online

Visit these Web sites to learn more about disabled dogs:

www.eddieswheels.com

www.handicappedpets.com

www.orthopets.com

www.rollingdogfarm.org

www.therapaw.com

Index

About the Author

Meish Goldish has written more than 200 books for children. His book *Heart-Stopping Roller Coasters* was a Children's Choices Selection in 2011. He lives in Brooklyn, New York.